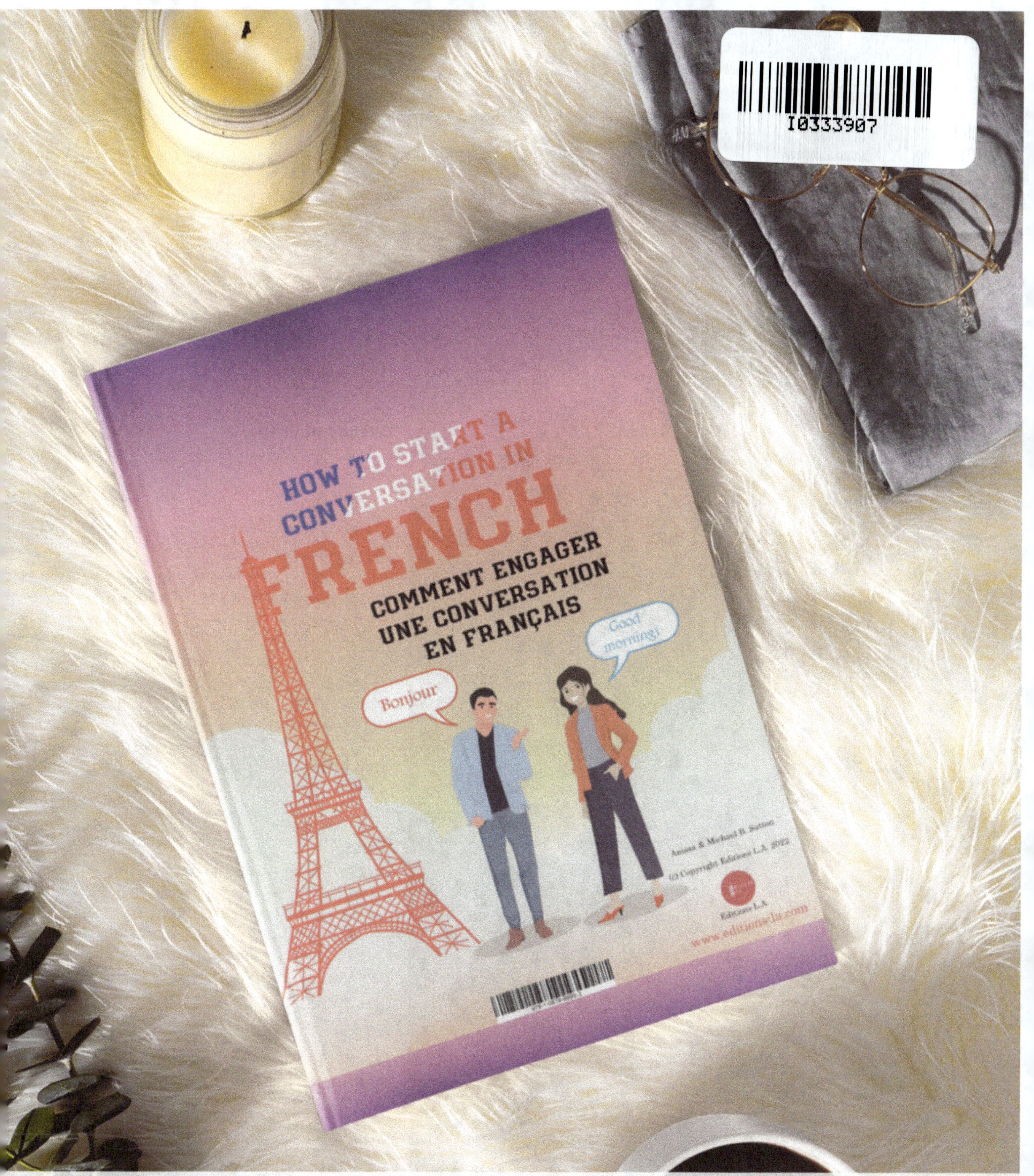
HOW TO START A CONVERSATION IN
FRENCH
COMMENT ENGAGER UNE CONVERSATION EN FRANÇAIS
Bonjour
Good morning!
www.editions-la.com

CONTENTS

Wendy Dale Young!
p. 06

Photos by Anissa Sutton
Make up & Hair By Sierra Kohn

06
WENDY DALE YOUNG
An Iconic Figure in Entertainment Industry, Celebrating Jazz Month Appreciation with her Smooth Jazz Rendition of "The Look of Love" and Daughter of Alan Young, Star of "Mister Ed Show

5
Editor's Note

06-09
Wendy Dale Young
From Dog Mom to Singer Wendy Dale Young's Jazzy Rendition of "The Look of Love" Will Steal Your Heart!

10 - 15
INTERVIEWS
Music Promoter **Jimi Wang and Translator Yu Yong Li** on Seymour Stein's Autobiography Tour Book Exhibition in China

JJ Hudson: How did Jmojii empower women through music and philanthropy after overcoming homelessness?

Drivetime: Meet Bernie C.: Jazz Musician, Composer, and KPIU Radio Host

16 - 23
JAZZY PAWS & JAZZ MONTH
- Purrfect Practice: Yoga with Your Cat
- Jazzing Up Your Playlist
- Books For Pets Lovers
- Pawesome Dining in L.A.
- Claw-some Films - Must-See Movies Featuring Adorable Dogs!

24-25
FASHION TIPS FOR A CONFIDENT YOU!
Hiding Your Belly With Style

26-27
Top Anti-Aging Tips
Feed Your Beauty:
Boost Skin & Hair With Nutrition & Supplements

28-29
Top Branding Tips
Simple Steps to Craft Your Artist Brand

30-31
BE A HERO FOR HOMELESS DOGS:
How You Can Help Animal Rescues in Need

PUMP IT UP MAGAZINE
LINKS

WEBSITE
www.pumpitupmagazine.com

FACEBOOK
www.facebook.com/pumpitupmagazine

TWITTER
www.twitter.com/pumpitupmag

SOUNDCLOUD
www.soundcloud.com/pumpitupmagazine

INSTAGRAM
pumpitupmagazine

PINTEREST
www.pinterest.com/pumpitupmagazine

PUMP IT UP MAGAZINE
30721 Russell Ranch Road
Suite 140
Westlake Village,
California 91362
United States

 (818)514 – 0038(Ext:102)
 info@pumpitupmagazine.com

EDITORIAL

Greeting Readers!

We are thrilled to present to you a special edition of our magazine, dedicated to celebrating our beloved pets and the appreciation of jazz music.

In this issue, we have curated a selection of articles and features that highligh the bond between humans and their furry companions.
From Purrfect Practice: Yoga with Your Cat to must-see movies featuring ador able dogs, we have something for every pet lover.

As we celebrate Jazz Month, we are excited to showcase
Wendy Dale Young, a jazz singer
whose story of following her passion will inspire you.
Her jazzy rendition of "The Look of Love"
is sure to steal your heart and leave you wanting more.

In addition, we have interviews with music industry insiders such as
JJ Hudson, Drivetime, and Jimi Wang & Yu Yong about Seymour Stein,
who share their experiences and insights .

But it's not just about entertainment and lifestyle. We also have articles on how you can help animal rescues in need and be a hero for homeless dogs.
As pet lovers, we have a responsibility
to make the world a better place for our furry friends.

We hope that this edition will bring a smile to your face and remind you of th joy that our pets and jazz music bring to our lives.

Thank you for joining us
on this journey of celebration and appreciation.

Warm regards,

Anissa Sutton

CONTRIBUTORS

FOUNDER
Anissa Sutton

EDITOR
Michael B. Sutton

FASHION
Tiffani Sutton

MUSIC JOURNALIST
Jimi Wang & Yu Yong

MARKETING
Grace Rose

PARTNERS

Editions L.A.
www.editions-la.com

The Sound Of L.A.
www.thesoundofla.com

Info Music
www.infomusic.fr

L.A. Unlimited
www.launlimitedinc.com

Wendy Dale Young
Reviving 'The Look of Love' Jazzily!

Wendy Dale Young's journey in the entertainment industry has been nothing short of extraordinary. Born into an entertainment family in Los Angeles, California, Wendy's love for the arts was instilled at a young age. Her father, a British comedian, had his own variety show, "The Alan Young Show," in New York on radio and television. Wendy's family lived in England while her father worked on films and television, and in 1959, they moved back to the US when he was cast as Wilbur on the TV series 'Mister Ed'.

Wendy's career in the entertainment industry has been varied and multifaceted. She began her journey dancing with the Bolshoi Ballet and later went on to work on Broadway and the West End. Her talent for identifying and cultivating emerging talent was showcased when she produced and promoted a Southern Kitchen musical, "The Right Smart of Love!," which brought innovative and thought-provoking works to audiences.

Despite her early success in the industry, Wendy faced several challenges along the way. She struggled with an underlying health condition that went undetected for years, which eventually forced her to quit performing altogether. This was a difficult time for Wendy, who struggled with depression and frustration. However, she was able to channel her passion and creativity into writing, which became a new source of inspiration and fulfillment.

Wendy's career highlights include writing her first book, "Behind the Eyes of Liberty Pearl," which is a true story about the miraculous rescue of a little dog and is all about love. She also wrote a musical that deals with a controversial subject and is all about love, and she hopes her work will bring about healing and acceptance of just being human.

In addition to her professional pursuits, Wendy is an avid traveler and a devoted animal lover. She often incorporates her experiences and passions into her creative work. Wendy has rescued and adopted many animals, which has become a new passion of hers.

Produced by former Motown producer Michael B. Sutton at The Sound of L.A., Wendy's smooth jazz cover of "The Look of Love" will be available for release in April, in celebration of Jazz Month Appreciation and International Pet Day. Wendy's rendition of the classic song promises to be a unique and soulful interpretation that will touch the hearts of listeners.

Wendy's journey in the entertainment industry has been one of resilience, creativity, and passion. She has inspired generations of artists and audiences alike, and her contributions to the arts and entertainment world have left an indelible mark. As we look forward to the release of her new work, we can only imagine what other beautiful creations Wendy has in store for us in the future.

WENDY DALE YOUNG'S

SMOOTH JAZZ COVER OF "THE LOOK OF LOVE" BRINGS NEW LIFE TO A CLASSIC SONG

WWW.WENDYDALEYOUNG.COM

Wendy Dale Young

Let's start by talking about this project that clearly holds a special place in your heart. Could you tell me more about what inspired you to create "Love, Larry" and why you believe it's an important story to share with audiences?

WENDY DALE YOUNG:
I'm excited to share my new musical, "Love, Larry," with you. Based on a true story!
The musical is a touching love story between a woman and a bisexual man, set against the backdrop of the day after John Lennon's murder in 1980.

Larry and Cindy fall deeply in love despite the challenges they face, including Larry's terminal illness and Cindy's struggle to accept his sexuality. Their story is told through letters, forming the foundation of a story that deals with the most difficult event any of us will experience - the death of a loved one.

I believe that "Love, Larry" is a story that will resonate with many people, as it deals with a controversial relationship that is still prevalent today. My intention is to produce a successful show, with the ultimate goal of bringing it to Broadway.

To achieve this, I am raising funds through GoFundMe to produce a staged reading and promote the show. This includes making song demos, hiring an engineer, musicians, and singers, charting the music, hiring a theatre, a director and choreographer, musical director, lighting person, 12 performers, musicians for the performance, paying for auditions, one week of rehearsal, performances, scripts, music, and fliers. If possible, I would also like to hire public relations to help spread the word about the show.

By supporting 'Love, Larry,' you're not just helping to bring a beautiful story to life - you're also investing in the power of the arts to inspire and uplift us all.

If you believe in the importance of the arts and would like to help me bring "Love, Larry" to life, please consider making a donation through my GoFundMe page:

www.gofundme.com/f/a-new-musical-love-larry.

Your contribution can make a real difference, and I'm grateful for any support you can provide.

Can you share with us a bit about your life and journey as a musician, and how it has led to your current project?

WENDY DALE YOUNG: My life has always been about music. As a young dancer, always inspired by the music. As my life unfolded so did my musical projects. Always inspired. The journey has taken me to from performing all genres from ballet, musical theatre, cabaret, rock n roll, to songwriting and recently I've written a Musical. Then most recent "The Look of Love." I am so grateful for my passion of music. Literally it has saved my life and got me through some serious turbulent times.

How has your entertainment family influenced your approach to music and the arts?

WENDY DALE YOUNG: I was born into creativity, performing and professionalism thanks to my parents. It totally inspired and influenced me as it's all I've known.

What inspired you to create a smooth jazz cover of "The Look of Love"?

WENDY DALE YOUNG: I have always loved this song. As a little girl I heard Dusty Springfield's version. I was haunted. So simple and powerful.

April is Jazz Appreciation Month. How do you feel about the role of jazz music in contemporary culture?

I believe the role of jazz music is so important in today's culture. Combining traditional jazz with smooth jazz may offer more of a sophisticated bridge to today's music and to younger listeners that they may relate to.

What drives your creative curiosity and exploration across different genres and mediums?

WENDY DALE YOUNG: I'm just wired that way! Passion fuels my ideas, and even the smallest things can inspire me to create something new. I never tire of being inspired.

Pump it up Magazine / 09- 34

Interview

JJ HUDSON
multi-talented artist and musician philanthropist

Photographer: Brandon Kruszeniak - Arizonia

JJ Hudson, also known as Jmojii, is a rising multi-talented artist based in Seattle who blends old and new school rap, classical music, and EDM to create a unique style of music that empowers all genders through her life experiences. In this interview, JJ shares insights on her distinctive blend of genres, the challenges of being a female artist, and her involvement in philanthropic work. She also discusses her upcoming projects and her inspiring message of self-acceptance and empowerment.

Can you explain your unique style of blending old and new school rap, classical music, and EDM?

JJ HUDSON: I'm a little old school mixed with new school, and I love classical music, as well as EDM! And any music with passion and deep meaning will always grab me.

What challenges have you faced as a female artist in the music industry, and how have you overcome them?

JJ HUDSON: I worry about being judged negatively based on my appearance and gender, but it's more of a self-created factor, as it is basic insecurity as a woman in a world where people can be extremely cruel and judgmental. I have also faced some people who were really only interested in helping if I paid them.

How has your music inspired and empowered women, and how do you plan to continue that message in your future work?

JJ HUDSON: Hopefully, my life experiences, good and bad, and my efforts to overcome will inspire women and everyone will help them through whatever dark moments they may be facing.

What sets you apart from other artists?

JJ HUDSON: My ability to play the piano in multiple, unique styles, combined with my ability to rap and sing and that I love many genres of music, I think those elements may add to my distinction as an artist.

What message do you hope to convey through your work?

JJ HUDSON: Be fearless, original, and mindful of your influence on others. Don't aspire to be something others want you to be, rather, stay true to yourself and live the best life you can.

Interview

Can you tell us more about your involvement with Runway to Freedom?

JJ HUDSON: My cousin is a survivor from domestic violence and she started Runway to Freedom to give a safe place for people escaping domestic violence, providing resources and a runway show that displays the beauty and strength of the survivor.

Who are some of your biggest musical influences, and how have they inspired your music?

JJ HUDSON: I grew up listening to a lot of 90s music on the radio or on cassette. I remember when KUBE 93 and KCMU started playing rap, and I would press record on my cassette to catch a song I liked and then I'd practice the lyrics.

What can fans expect from you in the future, and what are some of your upcoming projects?

JJ HUDSON: I have several projects I'm working on, including a song for an incredible and inspiring MMA fighter, a new single called "Why Why Why" featuring Jdore & produced by Robbie Rob, and a podcast called "Voices From The 4th City."

What advice or words of inspiration would you give to women who want to pursue a career in the music industry?

JJ HUDSON: It's important to not live in fear, trust the development process, stay original and true to who you are by being you and not anyone else, but don't be afraid to show and adopt elements of the artists who inspire you. And most importantly, believe in yourself and be willing to work hard. Remember, "hard work beats talent when talent refuses to work hard."

How do you plan to celebrate International Pet Day on April 11th?

JJ HUDSON: I'm excited for International Pet Day! Springtime in Seattle is beautiful, and I love taking Mr. Moose for walks and dressing him up.
He's been a huge part of my recovery and therapy for my PTSD, so I'll be giving him lots of love today.
Plus, everyone loves Mr. Moose!

Check out JJ Hudson's social media profiles and listen to her original track "Let It Pop" on YouTube, as well as her music on major streaming platforms. Visit her website and learn about her involvement in Runway to Freedom with Lauren Grinnell. Don't forget to follow her for updates and more content!

Instagram: @iamjjhudson
Facebook: /IamJMojii
TikTok: @iamjjhudson
YouTube: @Iamjjhudson
Website: https://jjhudson.online/
Runway to Freedom: https://runwaytofreedom.org/

KEVIN NANCE (Sikjitsu fighter and now co-promoter for Excitefight) – JJ HUDSON – Ethan Child (Sikjitsu MMA fighter) – GRANDMIXER GMS

JJ Hudson (Jmojii) and her group, including Nes, Larisa Krutik (model), George Torres (DJ Solar), Robert Brewer (Actor and DJ Forrest Gump), and Grandmixer GMS, pose with Bruce Lee's favorite restaurant, Tai Tung Restaurant in Seattle. They even sat at the table where Bruce Lee used to sit right behind them

JJ Hudson (Jmojii) and her furry friend, Mr. Moose, pose for a photo in front of the Bruce Lee tribute material at Tai Tung Restaurant in Seattle. Jacquelyn Hudson notes that JJ is wearing a High Children shirt in the picture.

JJ Hudson (Jmojii) and her mom pose for a photo, with her mom wearing a Pump It Up Magazine t-shirt featuring the cover where JJ Hudson and her group, The High Children, graced the front cover

Bernie C.

**Jazz Musician and KPIU Radio Host:
An Interview with a Smooth Jazz Expert**

Meet a talented musician and radio host who has dedicated his life to the world of jazz. With decades of experience as a percussionist, composer, and band leader, he has a wealth of knowledge and stories to share about his career in the music industry. As a radio hos for KPIU RADIO - Pump it up magazine Official Radio Station, he brings the latest and greatest in smooth jazz to his listeners, while also providing a platform for up-and-coming artists to showcase their talents. In this interview, we delve into his journey as a jazz musician, the challenges he's faced along the way, and his thoughts on Jazz Month and the enduring appeal of jazz music.

What inspired your jazz and radio career, and how did you start in the industry?

BERNIE C.: My dad introduced me to music at a young age and took me to gigs where I played drums. At 15, I watched a famous DJ do his radio shows, which sparked my interest in broadcasting. I joined a band in my 20s and learned to play jazz, which led to my career in jazz music.

What is your band Drivetime's music style, and how do you create new pieces?

BERNIE C.: Drivetime plays fusion, funk, and Latin jazz, and I use percussion to create motifs and find chord structures to build melodies. We write what we want and create a unique sound without industry restrictions.

How do you select music for your radio show, and what can listeners expect?

BERNIE C.: In my radio show, I aim to bring my listeners the best of smooth jazz while also providing a platform for emerging artists within the genre. Rather than solely relying on the Smooth Jazz Network's weekly chart, I also search for new releases and tracks from fresh talent to feature on my show. I'm passionate about promoting diversity and believe in showcasing a range of music for my listeners. Additionally, I've had the pleasure of discovering some talented artists through Pump It Up Magazine, which has been an exciting opportunity to bring new and unique music to my audience.

How do you celebrate Jazz Month, and what does it mean to you?

BERNIE C.: Jazz Month holds a special place in my heart, as it is a time to celebrate the beauty and diversity of jazz music. During this month, I take the opportunity to honor the success of my friends and associates in the industry, and I conduct interviews with notable jazz musicians for my radio show during events like the Berks Jazz Fest.

How does Jazz Month help to promote and celebrate the jazz genre, and what can fans expect from your radio show and band during this month?

Jazz has diverse styles: Bebop, Straight Ahead, Fusion, Latin Jazz. My radio show airs mostly Smooth Jazz, but my band, Bernie C., plays Urban Organic Jazz. Unlike solo artists who use backing tracks on the road, we don't. I play the hottest artists that are crusin up the charts on my consistent radio show.

What are some of your memorable experiences during Jazz Month, and what made those experiences special to you?

Every month is Jazz month to me, but highlights include playing at the 2017 Tony Awards in Times Square with Justin Guarini & Debora Cox, writing our first single, Gettin' Witit, with Bob Baldwin, and being nominated for the HMMA for our jazz reimagining of California Dreamin.

Why do you think Jazz is an important and enduring genre, and why does it resonate with audiences around the world?

Jazz is the music of the human condition turned into joy. It tells a personal story that we all can feel the pain, the joy, the sorrow. And the structured/un-structured nature of jazz allows a soloist to express and go anywhere in the universe, taking the audience right with them. Music is the universal language.

What challenges do jazz musicians and radio hosts face today, and how do you navigate those challenges in your career?

My career in music is dented with failures, personnel changes in the band, canceled gigs (during Covid), and some degree of rejection. The best way to deal with these issues is to keep moving forward, never let anyone see you sweat. Don't make music, be music.

What advice would you give to aspiring jazz musicians and radio hosts looking to make a name for themselves in the industry, especially during Jazz Month?

Be real and believe in yourself. If you can't enjoy what you're doing, find something else. Start young, study hard, practice harder, and perfect your craft. If you're going into broadcasting, know the music and artists you're playing. Love what you're doing, and success will follow.

What upcoming projects do you have in the works, and what can fans expect from you in the coming months?

With my band Drivetime, we have produced two brand new CDs, a total of 17 original tunes. We've already released 3 singles from the first CD, Un Domani Migliore (A Better Tomorrow), and the second is still nameless. Both CDs are slated for release this summer. We invited award-winning Yulia Petrova to play on our next single, I Can't Forget You, and Andrew Neu joins us on a number of tunes on both CDs. For more information, please visit: www.drivetimeuoj.com

Interview

Seymour Stein, founder of Sire label, discovered Madonna, The Ramones & Talking Heads. His autobiography "My Life in Music" caused a frenzy in China in 2022. Jimi Wang & Yu Yong Li toured the book across 9 cities, inviting local musicians to perform classics from the book. The tour will relaunch in March with an exclusive interview. Learn about the man behind the music legend.

JIMI WANG & YU YONG: We wrote to Seymour Stein, the author, after the book was published in Europe and the US, and he agreed. It took four years to be published in China due to translation, the pandemic, and approval processes. But it was worth it.

Why is the book more influential in China than in the US and Europe?

JIMI WANG & YU YONG: In the 1990s, overproduced records were exported to China as plastic waste, giving young Chinese access to rock and pop music. Seymour's record label, Sire, was popular and left an impact on people's memories.

How's the tour going?

JIMI WANG & YU YONG: The tour began in August and we went to nine cities, but limited capacity due to the pandemic. We had to suspend events in December due to a virus outbreak. We hope to continue the tour and visit 20 cities in China.

Your tour is creative, playing the songs from the book. Is this interesting?

JIMI WANG & YU YONG: Yes, our translator suggested using a concert format in bookstores, creating a wonderful combination of music and culture. We collaborate with local musicians, adding excitement.

Can you comment on Seymour Stein?

JIMI WANG & YU YONG: Seymour developed an independent record label into a world-famous music label, changing the trend of pop music. He advocates for the spirit of inheritance, an inspiration to everyone in the music industry.

Are there any plans to expand the tour to other countries?

JIMI WANG & YU YONG: Our focus is on completing the tour in China and promoting the book. We received inquiries from publishers in other Asian countries, and we're considering expanding the tour. We believe Seymour's story has a universal appeal.

Are you a songwriter or composer struggling to protect your work and releases?
Well Bernie Capodici has done all the work for you in his new book
"Modern Recording Artist Handbook, How To Guide Simplified"

Only $12.95

MUST READ FOR INDEPENDENT ARTISTS

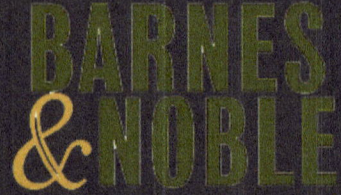

KINDLE $9.99 - HARDCOVER $22.95 - PAPERBACK $12.95

YOGA WITH YOUR CAT

Find Your Inner Feline with Purrfect Practice

Yoga has long been known for its calming benefits, but did you know that incorporating your furry feline friend can enhance your yoga experience? That's right – cat yoga, or "cat-ssisted" yoga, is a growing trend that allows you to deepen your mind-body connection while spending quality time with your beloved pet. In honor of International Pet Day, we've compiled a guide on how to practice yoga with your cat for a purrfect wellness routine.

BENEFITS OF CAT YOGA

Helps reduce stress and anxiety
Improves flexibility and balance
Strengthens the bond between you and your cat
Provides a fun and playful way to exercise
Promotes relaxation and inner peace

PREPARING FOR CAT YOGA

Choose a quiet and comfortable space for you and your cat to practice in
Use a non-slip mat to prevent injuries
Have toys or treats nearby to keep your cat engaged and focused
Ensure that your cat is willing to participate – forcing them can cause stress and anxiety

CAT YOGA POSES

Cat-Cow: Start on your hands and knees with your cat nearby. Inhale as you arch your back and look up, then exhale as you round your spine and tuck your chin to your chest. Repeat for several breaths.

Downward Dog: From the Cat-Cow pose, tuck your toes under and lift your hips up and back. Keep your knees slightly bent and your heels reaching towards the floor. Your cat may choose to walk underneath you or hang out nearby.

Seated Twist: Sit cross-legged with your cat in front of you. Inhale as you lengthen your spine, then exhale as you twist towards your cat, gently placing your hand on their back. Repeat on the other side.

Warrior II: Stand with your feet hip-width apart and your cat nearby. Step your left foot back and turn it out, then bend your right knee and extend your arms out to the sides. Gaze over your right hand as you hold the pose for several breaths. Repeat on the other side.

TIPS FOR A SUCCESSFUL CAT YOGA SESSION

Follow your cat's lead – they may choose to participate or simply observe
Allow your cat to approach you on their own terms
Use positive reinforcement with treats and praise
Don't force your cat into any poses – they will naturally move and stretch on their own.

Cat yoga is a wonderful way to improve your physical and mental well-being while bonding with your furry friend.

Give it a try and see how the purrfect practice can benefit you and your cat.
Happy International Pet Day!

KPIU RADIO
THE WEST COAST WAVE

MUST-PLAY ESSENTIAL RECORDS

#20 The 3 Keys - That Beat
#19 Ragan Whiteside - Full Court Press
#18 Paul Brown - 7 and 7
Featured Artist - Yulia - Two Rivers
#17 Paula Atherton - Open Road
#16 Riley Richard - Superstar
#15 Kim Scott - Off The Top
*Jazz Discover - Jeff Goldblum
f / Freda Payne - Lazy Afternoon*
#14 Lindsey Webster - I'm Ok
#13 Roberto Restuccia - Stand Up
#12 Maysa - I Don't Mind
*Spotlight - Aneessa & Michael B Sutton
"I Found Myself In You"*
#11 Phylicia Rae - Now Or Never
#10 Jazz Holdouts - Piermont Nights
#09 Najee - Bounce
*Featured Artist - The Verve Jazz Ensemble
"Once I Loved"*
#08 Paul Taylor - And Now This
#07 Nils - Night In The Algarve
#06 Darren Rahn - Everlasting
Featured Artist - JC Sol - Our Groove
#05 David P. Stevens - After Party
#04 Ryan La Valette - Loves Melody
#03 Rick Braun - Turkish
Featured Artist - Drivetime - Un Domani Migliore
#02 Blake Aaron - Crush
#01 Jimmy B. - It's Personal
Outro - JJ Sansaverino - Ride With Me

WWW.KPIURADIO.COM

**Everyday 7pm-9pm (PST) -10PM-12PM(EST)
hosted by Bernie C. on KPIURADIO.COM**

The Verve Jazz Ensemble - www.Verve-Jazz.com

April is Jazz Appreciation Month, the perfect opportunity to add some smooth jazz tunes to your playlist. Jazz music has been known to have a calming effect on the mind and body, helping to reduce stress and anxiety. Certain frequencies in jazz music have been found to be especially beneficial for relaxation and healing. Here's a breakdown of some of the healing frequencies found in jazz music:

432 Hz: This frequency is said to resonate with the heart chakra, promoting healing and balance in the body. Many jazz songs are tuned to this frequency, making it a great choice for relaxation and meditation.
528 Hz: Also known as the "love frequency," this frequency is believed to promote healing, peace, and positivity. Jazz songs tuned to this frequency can help reduce stress and anxiety, and promote a sense of calm and well-being.
639 Hz: This frequency is said to promote emotional healing and harmony in relationships. Listening to jazz music tuned to this frequency can help improve communication and foster positive relationships.

Incorporating these healing frequencies into your jazz playlist can help enhance the benefits of jazz music for your overall well-being. And where better to find great jazz tunes than on KPIU Radio's Top 20 Smooth Jazz Chart from The Drivetime Show by Bernie C.? Broadcasting daily from 7pm PST to 9pm PST at www.kpiuradio.com, KPIU is the official radio of Pump It Up Magazine and is dedicated to discovering jazz and smooth jazz gems every week and playing the main famous stars in that genre.

Whether you're looking to reduce stress and anxiety, improve your emotional well-being, or simply enjoy some smooth tunes, jazz music can provide the perfect soundtrack. Add some smooth jazz tunes to your playlist this Jazz Appreciation Month and experience the healing benefits of this iconic music genre.

If you're not sure where to start, consider checking out "Once I Loved" by the Verve Jazz Ensemble, featured on KPIU Radio's Top 20 Smooth Jazz Chart. This upbeat and swinging tune is a modern interpretation of the classic Brazilian jazz standard by Antonio Carlos Jobim and is sure to add some energy and joy to your playlist.

Take some time this Jazz Appreciation Month to jazz up your playlist and experience the healing benefits of this iconic music genre. Whether you're tuning in to KPIU Radio or exploring new artists and frequencies on your own, jazz music is sure to provide a soothing and uplifting experience for your mind, body, and soul.

BOOKS FOR PETS LOVERS
Celebrate International Pet Day
with These Must-Read Books About Our Furry Friends!

Pets have been our loyal companions, protectors, and sources of joy for centuries. They have also inspired us to write about them, and to share their stories, wisdom, and love with the world. That's why on International Pet Day, we want to celebrate our furry friends by recommending some of the best books about them. Whether you are a cat person, a dog person, or a pet lover in general, these books will warm your heart, enrich your mind, and deepen your bond with your pet.

"Behind the Eyes of Liberty Pearl by Wendy Dale Young:

"Behind the Eyes of Liberty Pearl: The True Story of a Little White Puppy Found in the Rubble in Saddam Hussein's Detonated Baghdad Presidential Palace" by Wendy Dale Young: This heartwarming book tells the true story of a little dog named Liberty Pearl, who was rescued Rescued from Saddam Hussein's Baghdad Presidential Palace and was rehabilitated and lived in Los Angeles. It's a story about love, hope, and redemption, and shows how pets can bring out the best in us. The book also includes beautiful illustrations and a message of gratitude and kindness.

You can buy the book on Amazon here: https://www.amazon.com/Behind-Eyes-Liberty-Pearl-Presidential/dp/1726302768

"The Art of Racing in the Rain" by Garth Stein:

This bestselling novel is narrated by a dog named Enzo, who shares his thoughts, observations, and dreams with his human family. It's a poignant and funny story about love, loss, and loyalty, and shows how dogs can teach us about resilience, courage, and the power of the present moment. The book also inspired a movie adaptation, which you can watch with your pet.

You can buy the book on Amazon here: https://www.amazon.com/Art-Racing-Rain-Novel/dp/0061537969

"Dewey: The Small-Town Library Cat Who Touched the World" by Vicki Myron:

This charming memoir tells the true story of a cat named Dewey, who was found in a library book drop and became a beloved mascot and therapy cat for the town of Spencer, Iowa. It's a story about community, compassion, and the magic of cats, and shows how pets can bring people together and heal their hearts. The book also includes photos and testimonials from Dewey's fans.

You can buy the book on Amazon here: https://www.amazon.com/Dewey-Small-Town-Library-Touched-World/dp/0446407410

"Marley & Me" by John Grogan:

This bestselling memoir is a classic tale of a family and their mischievous but lovable Labrador retriever named Marley. It's a story about growing up, starting a family, and learning to love unconditionally, and shows how pets can teach us about patience, forgiveness, and the value of family. The book also inspired a movie adaptation, which you can watch with your pet.

You can buy the book on Amazon here: https://www.amazon.com/Marley-Me-Life-Love-Worlds/dp/0060817089

By reading these books, you can celebrate International Pet Day, honor our furry friends, and deepen your bond with your pet. You can also support pet rescue and advocacy organizations, such as the American Society for the Prevention of Cruelty to Animals (ASPCA), by donating, volunteering, or adopting a pet in need. So grab a book, snuggle with your pet, and let the magic of pets and books transform your day!

BOOKS FOR PETS LOVERS
Celebrate International Pet Day
with These Must-Read Books About Our Furry Friends!

Pets have been our loyal companions, protectors, and sources of joy for centuries. They have also inspired us to write about them, and to share their stories, wisdom, and love with the world. That's why on International Pet Day, we want to celebrate our furry friends by recommending some of the best books about them. Whether you are a cat person, a dog person, or a pet lover in general, these books will warm your heart, enrich your mind, and deepen your bond with your pet.

"Behind the Eyes of Liberty Pearl by Wendy Dale Young:

"Behind the Eyes of Liberty Pearl: The True Story of a Little White Puppy Found in the Rubble in Saddam Hussein's Detonated Baghdad Presidential Palace" by Wendy Dale Young: This heartwarming book tells the true story of a little dog named Liberty Pearl, who was rescued Rescued from Saddam Hussein's Baghdad Presidential Palace and was rehabilitated and lived in Los Angeles, became a beloved pet of a U.S. president. It's a story about love, hope, and redemption, and shows how pets can bring out the best in us. The book also includes beautiful illustrations and a message of gratitude and kindness.

You can buy the book on Amazon here: https://www.amazon.com/Behind-Eyes-Liberty-Pearl-Presidential/dp/1726302768

"The Art of Racing in the Rain" by Garth Stein:

This bestselling novel is narrated by a dog named Enzo, who shares his thoughts, observations, and dreams with his human family. It's a poignant and funny story about love, loss, and loyalty, and shows how dogs can teach us about resilience, courage, and the power of the present moment. The book also inspired a movie adaptation, which you can watch with your pet.

You can buy the book on Amazon here: https://www.amazon.com/Art-Racing-Rain-Novel/dp/0061537969

"Dewey: The Small-Town Library Cat Who Touched the World" by Vicki Myron:

This charming memoir tells the true story of a cat named Dewey, who was found in a library book drop and became a beloved mascot and therapy cat for the town of Spencer, Iowa. It's a story about community, compassion, and the magic of cats, and shows how pets can bring people together and heal their hearts. The book also includes photos and testimonials from Dewey's fans.

You can buy the book on Amazon here: https://www.amazon.com/Dewey-Small-Town-Library-Touched-World/dp/0446407410

"Marley & Me" by John Grogan:

This bestselling memoir is a classic tale of a family and their mischievous but lovable Labrador retriever named Marley. It's a story about growing up, starting a family, and learning to love unconditionally, and shows how pets can teach us about patience, forgiveness, and the value of family. The book also inspired a movie adaptation, which you can watch with your pet.

You can buy the book on Amazon here: https://www.amazon.com/Marley-Me-Life-Love-Worlds/dp/0060817089

By reading these books, you can celebrate International Pet Day, honor our furry friends, and deepen your bond with your pet. You can also support pet rescue and advocacy organizations, such as the American Society for the Prevention of Cruelty to Animals (ASPCA), by donating, volunteering, or adopting a pet in need. So grab a book, snuggle with your pet, and let the magic of pets and books transform your day!

CLAW-SOME MOVIES

International Pet Day is a special day dedicated to celebrating the bond between pets and their owners. What better way to celebrate this day than by watching some of the most memorable dog movies ever made? Whether you're in the mood for an adventure, a heartwarming drama, or a charming comedy, there's a dog movie out there for everyone. In this article, we'll take a look at some of the best dog movies to watch on International Pet Day.

"Homeward Bound: The Incredible Journey" (1993)
This classic film follows the adventures of three pets - a golden retriever, a bulldog, and a cat - as they embark on a dangerous journey through the wilderness to find their way back home. Along the way, they face many challenges and learn the true meaning of friendship, loyalty, and perseverance. "Homeward Bound" is a heartwarming tale that will make you laugh, cry, and cheer.

"Marley & Me" (2008)
Based on the bestselling memoir by John Grogan, "Marley & Me" tells the story of a couple who adopt a mischievous yellow Labrador retriever named Marley. Through ups and downs, joys and sorrows, Marley becomes an integral part of the family and teaches them the true meaning of love and devotion. This touching film is a must-see for anyone who has ever loved a dog.

"The Art of Racing in the Rain" (2019)
This heartwarming drama, based on the bestselling novel by Garth Stein, follows the story of Enzo, a wise and philosophical golden retriever who shares the life of his beloved owner, a race car driver. Through Enzo's eyes, we see the joys and sorrows of life, the power of love and family, and the unbreakable bond between humans and dogs. "The Art of Racing in the Rain" is a beautiful tribute to the special connection between dogs and their owners.

"Bolt" (2008)
This charming Disney animated film tells the story of a lovable dog named Bolt who thinks he has superpowers and must save his owner from danger. Along the way, he learns about the true meaning of courage, friendship, and identity. With adorable characters, witty humor, and stunning animation, "Bolt" is a must-see for dog lovers of all ages.

Watching a dog movie is a great way to spend quality time with your furry friend and appreciate the unique relationship you share. So grab some snacks, cuddle up with your pet, and enjoy a Pawsome Films marathon!

HIDING YOUR BELLY WITH STYLE
Fashion Tips For A Confident You!

Belly fat can be a source of insecurity for many people, regardless of their gender or age. It can also be a challenge when it comes to finding clothes that fit well and flatter your body shape.
However, with some smart styling and shopping, you can hide your belly and feel confident and fashionable. Here are some fashion tips that work for both men and women:

Choose the right fit: The most important rule when it comes to hiding your belly is to choose clothes that fit you well, but not too tight or too loose. Opt for clothes that skim your body without being too clingy or baggy, and avoid clothes that are too small or too big. You can also try layering with a lightweight and flowy jacket or cardigan to add some coverage and dimension.

Look for vertical lines: They can create the illusion of length and slimness, and draw the eye away from your belly. Look for clothes that have vertical details, such as pinstripes, ribbed knits, or vertical seams. You can also try layering with a long scarf or necklace to create a vertical line.

Avoid horizontal lines: Horizontal lines can emphasize your belly and create a widening effect. Avoid clothes that have wide horizontal stripes, color blocks, or patterns. Instead, look for clothes that have small and subtle patterns, or solid colors that are dark or muted.

Accessorize strategically: Accessories can be a great way to add some style and personality to your outfit, but it's important to choose them strategically. Avoid accessories that draw attention to your belly, such as belts or waist packs. Instead, choose accessories that draw attention to your face or upper body, such as hats, sunglasses, or scarves.

Embrace shapewear: Shapewear can be a secret weapon when it comes to hiding your belly and creating a smooth silhouette. Look for shapewear that is comfortable, breathable, and fits well. You can also try layering with a camisole or tank top to provide some extra support and coverage.

By following these fashion tips, you can hide your belly and feel confident and stylish.
Remember, fashion is not about hiding your flaws, but highlighting your strengths and expressing your personality!

Funk Therapy

| Funky | Trendy | Cool | Hip |

Wear The Music You Love!

Visit our merchandise store on our website:

WWW.FUNKTHERAPYMUSIC.COM

10% Discount code: STAYFUNKY

- Hoodies
- Crop Top
- Sweat Pants
- Bucket Hats
- Slides
- Mugs

UNISEX T-SHIRTS

Brown T-Shirt

GRAB IT NOW

Orange T-Shirt

GRAB IT NOW

Beige T-Shirts

GRAB IT NOW

Join our community
@funktherapy2

TOP ANTI-AGING TIPS
Feed Your Beauty

As we age, our skin and hair can start to show signs of wear and tear, but by incorporating the right nutrients into our diets, we can help slow down the aging process and maintain healthy, youthful-looking skin and hair. One powerful ingredient to consider adding to your routine is **black seed oil.** This oil has been used for centuries in traditional medicine and has been found to have numerous health benefits, including anti-inflammatory and antioxidant properties that can help fight the signs of aging.

In addition **to black seed oil,** there are several other foods that are great for anti-aging.(Buy now at www.WestEndOrganix.com). Here are a few to consider adding to your diet:

Berries
Berries are packed with antioxidants, which help fight off free radicals that can cause damage to the skin and accelerate the aging process. Blueberries, raspberries, and strawberries are all great options.

Fatty fish
Fatty fish like salmon, tuna, and mackerel are rich in omega-3 fatty acids, which help keep the skin hydrated and supple. Omega-3s also have anti-inflammatory properties, which can help reduce the appearance of fine lines and wrinkles.

Leafy greens
Leafy greens like spinach and kale are rich in vitamins A and C, which help promote healthy skin and collagen production. Collagen is essential for maintaining the elasticity and firmness of the skin, which can help reduce the appearance of fine lines and wrinkles.

Nuts
Nuts like almonds, walnuts, and cashews are rich in vitamin E, which is an antioxidant that helps protect the skin from damage caused by UV rays and environmental pollutants. Vitamin E also helps keep the skin moisturized and can help reduce the appearance of fine lines and wrinkles.

Dark chocolate
Dark chocolate is rich in flavonoids, which are antioxidants that help protect the skin from damage caused by free radicals. Flavonoids also help improve circulation, which can help promote healthy, glowing skin.

Avocado is packed with healthy fats and vitamin E, which help keep the skin moisturized and reduce the appearance of fine lines and wrinkles. Avocado also contains antioxidants that can help protect the skin from damage caused by free radicals.

Green tea
Green tea is rich in antioxidants called catechins, which have been shown to help improve skin elasticity and reduce the appearance of fine lines and wrinkles. Green tea also has anti-inflammatory properties, which can help soothe irritated skin.

Turmeric
Turmeric is a spice that has been used in traditional medicine for centuries. It contains curcumin, which has anti-inflammatory and antioxidant properties that can help protect the skin from damage and reduce the appearance of fine lines and wrinkles.

Sweet potatoes
Sweet potatoes are rich in beta-carotene, which is converted to vitamin A in the body. Vitamin A is essential for maintaining healthy skin and promoting cell turnover, which can help reduce the appearance of fine lines and wrinkles. Sweet potatoes also contain vitamin C, which helps promote collagen production and keep the skin looking firm and youthful.

All of these anti-aging foods can also be used as supplements in addition to being incorporated into your diet.

WEST END ORGANIX

Ageless Beauty, Organic Health

BLACK SEED OIL

HEALTHY IMMUNE SYSTEM
INFLAMMATORY RESPONSE

www.westendorganix.com

TOP BRANDING TIPS
Simple Steps to Craft Your Artist Brand

If you're an artist looking to establish a strong brand identity, you're in the right place. Crafting a memorable and effective brand is essential to standing out in the crowded art market and attracting new clients and collectors. In this article, we'll take a look at some top branding tips to help you create a cohesive and compelling artist brand.

Define your brand personality
Before you can start crafting your brand, you need to define what you want it to convey. Think about the personality you want your brand to have. Is it playful and whimsical? Serious and contemplative? Edgy and experimental? Once you have a clear idea of your brand personality, you can start to craft your visual identity and messaging.

Develop a consistent visual identity
Your visual identity should reflect your brand personality and be consistent across all of your marketing materials, including your website, social media, business cards, and promotional materials. This includes your logo, color palette, typography, and imagery. Use these elements consistently to create a cohesive and memorable brand identity.

Create compelling messaging
Your messaging should be clear and concise, and reflect your brand personality and values. Develop a tagline or mission statement that succinctly captures what sets you apart as an artist. Use this messaging consistently across all of your marketing materials to reinforce your brand identity.

Use social media to your advantage
Social media can be a powerful tool for building your brand and reaching new audiences. Choose the platforms that align with your brand personality and target audience, and use them consistently to showcase your work, share your story, and engage with your followers.

Collaborate with other brands
Collaborating with other artists or brands can be a great way to expand your reach and build your brand. Look for opportunities to collaborate on projects or events that align with your brand values and target audience.

Be authentic
At the end of the day, the most important aspect of your brand is authenticity. Be true to yourself and your artistic vision, and let your personality shine through in your branding. Your authenticity will help you stand out in a crowded market and attract the right clients and collectors.

Crafting a strong artist brand is crucial for success in the music industry. Not only does it help you stand out from the competition, but it also enables you to connect with your audience and build a lasting career. If you're an artist looking to take your brand to the next level, there are several branding and consulting agencies that can help.

One such agency is **Editions L.A. (www.editions-la.com).** Specializing in creating visually stunning identities and branding strategies for artists, musicians, and creative professionals, their team of experts can help you transform your artistic vision into a cohesive and impactful brand that resonates with your audience. With a focus on storytelling and collaboration, Editions L.A. offers customized solutions that engage and inspire.

Another option to consider is **Your Music Consultant (www.yourmusicconsultant.com).** Their team of experts provides personalized coaching and consulting services to help artists build successful and sustainable careers in the music industry. Whether you need help with branding, marketing, touring, or artist development, Your Music Consultant offers a wide range of services to help you achieve your goals and reach your full potential.

Crafting a strong artist brand takes time and effort, but it's essential to building a successful and sustainable career as an artist.

Editions L.A.

DIGITAL CREATIVE AGENCY

We Transform Your Vision Into Creative Results

Editions L.A. is a full-service agency based in Los Angeles. Our company is a collective of amazing people striving to build delightful services
We believe that is all about getting your message across clearly and with a "Wow!" thrown in for good measure.

Our Awesome Services

Branding

We build, style and tone your brand identity from the ground up.
We rebrand established bands, brands or businesses.

Merchandise Store
Website design and E-Commerce
Website updates

Digital Marketing

CD Cover | Banners | Logo design | Flyers | Brochures | Leaflets | Print ads | Magazine covers & artworks
Facebook / twitter / instagram / youtube artworks
| Book cover
Infographics | Icon Design |
| TshirtsProduct Labels | Presentation slides
Corporate graphics
Professional photo editing & enhancing
Redesign existing elements
YouTube Optimization and Monetization
Youtube Video Editing
Lyric Video and Advertising Design.

Publishing

BOOK COVER DESIGN
EBOOK FORMATTING SERVICES
and distribution on major platforms
(Amazon, Barnes & Nobles..)

Tell us about your dream and we will make it true!

Editions L.A.
7210 Jordan Avenue Suite B42, Canoga Park, California 91303, United States
info@edtions-la.com
Website: www.editions-la.com

YOUR MUSIC CONSULTANT

"You Believe And So Do We"

YOUR MUSIC CONSULTANT

"YOU BELIEVE, SO DO WE!"

We Can Help You To Grow Your Business

We are a monthly based service, we put faith in artists who has major potential, believed in them, and who are willing to spend their time and own money to work with us in building a successful music career!

Digital Marketing Services

SOCIAL MEDIA - STREAMING SERVICES - MUSIC DISTRIBUTION - PRESS RELEASE - PRESS DISTRIBUTION - PR

Radio Airplay and TV Commercial

TERRESTRIAL AND DIGITAL RADIO CAMPAIGN AL GENRES EXCEPT HEAVY METAL - CABLE TV AND MAJOR NETWORK COMMERCIAL

Licensing & Booking

CONCERTS, LIVE MUSIC, EVENTS, CLUB NIGHTS - RED CARPETS - FOREIGN LICENSING AND SUBOPUBLISHING

Why Choose Us ?

3 DECADES OF MUSIC BUSINESS EXPERIENCE
Platinium and Gold Records
MOTOWN RECORDS
UNIVERSAL
SONY
CAPITOL RECORDS

WE WORKED WITH:
Kanye West - Jay Z - Stevie Wonder - Michael Jackson - Germaine Jackson - Smokey Robinson - Dionne Warwick - Cheryl Lynn - The Originals -

📞 **1-818-514-0038**
(Ext. 1)
Monday - Friday / 9am to 6pm

FIND US :

www.YourMusicConsultant.com
30721 Russell Ranch Road Suite 140 Westlake Village, USA
Email : info@yourmusicconsultant.com

ANEESSA
MICHAEL B. SUTTON

I FOUND MYSELF IN YOU

OUT NOW

WWW.THESOUNDOFLA.COM

*Smooth Jazz Love Song
for An Essential Romantic Playlist
Capturing the joyful essence of
what it feels like
to love and be loved!*

MAKING A DIFFERENCE:
How You Can Help Animal Rescues in Need

If you're passionate about animal welfare, there are many ways you can make a difference and support these organizations. Here's how:

Volunteer your time:

Animal rescues rely on volunteers to help with a wide range of tasks, from walking dogs and socializing cats to organizing fundraisers and events. Whether you have a few hours a week or a few days a month, your time and skills can make a big difference. Check out websites like VolunteerMatch or Petfinder to find animal rescue organizations in your area that need volunteers.

Donate money:

Animal rescues are always in need of financial support to cover the cost of food, medical care, and other expenses. Even a small donation can go a long way in helping these organizations provide for the animals in their care. Consider donating to organizations like the ASPCA, Humane Society, or Best Friends Animal Society.

Foster an animal:

Fostering is a crucial part of the animal rescue process, as it provides temporary homes for animals in need. By opening up your home to a foster animal, you can help ease the burden on overcrowded shelters and give an animal a chance to thrive in a loving environment. Check with your local animal rescue organizations to see if they offer fostering opportunities, or look into organizations like Foster Dogs NYC or Petco Love.

Adopt an animal:

If you're looking to add a furry friend to your family, consider adopting from an animal rescue. By adopting, you not only give an animal a loving home but also help to make space for more animals in need. Check out websites like Petfinder or Adopt-a-Pet to find adoptable animals near you.

Spread the word:

One of the most powerful ways you can help animal rescues is by spreading the word about their work and the animals they have available for adoption. Share their social media posts, attend their events, and encourage others to get involved. Follow animal rescue organizations on social media platforms like Instagram or Facebook and share their posts with your friends and family.

By taking action and supporting animal rescues, you can help make a difference in the lives of animals in need. So why not take the first step today and find a way to get involved?

Links for ways to help:

VolunteerMatch: https://www.volunteermatch.org/
Petfinder: https://www.petfinder.com/volunteer/
ASPCA: https://www.aspca.org/donate
Humane Society: https://www.humanesociety.org/donate
Best Friends Animal Society: https://bestfriends.org/donate
Foster Dogs NYC: https://fosterdogsnyc.com/foster-a-dog/
Petco Love: https://www.petcolove.org/
Petfinder (adoptable animals): https://www.petfinder.com/
Adopt-a-Pet: https://www.adoptapet.com/

www.ingramcontent.com/pod-product-compliance
Lightning Source LLC
Chambersburg PA
CBHW080902010526
44118CB00015B/2235